THE FEVER OF BEING

THE FEVER OF BEING

poems by

Luis Alberto Urrea

West End Press

I owe a special debt of gratitude to Lorna Dee Cervantes, without whose help this book would not exist in its present form.

Some of these poems first appeared, in part or in their entirety, in *AGNI, Cedar Rock, Literatura Fronteriza, Maize, The Mind's Eye, Sequoyah*; thanks to editors one and all.

Along with the usual suspects in Boulder, I must thank: Nina DeGramont, Michael Dorsey, Jay Griswold, Jen Kemper, Jennifer Klein, Christal McDougall, Melinda MacInnes, Roberta Maldonado, Mark Saunders, and Mark "Ina Gadda Da Vida" Spitzer. You helped me become a better writer.

First edition, October 1994
ISBN 0-931122-78-3

Winner of the 1994 Western States Book Award for Poetry

The Western States Book Awards are a project of the Western States Arts Federation. The awards are supported by the Xerox Foundation, Crane Duplicating Services, and the Witter Bynner Foundation for Poetry. Additional funding is provided by the National Endowment for the Arts.

Cover photograph by Barbara Davis
Cover design by Michael Reed
Typography by Prototype, Albuquerque, NM

West End Press • P.O. Box 27334 • Albuquerque, New Mexico 87125

Contents

I. FIRST CONVOCATION

The Sunday Drive 3

II. PROCESSION

I Tried to Write A Poem About This
Once A Year for Thirteen Years 7

Abelino Garcia: A Song of My Elder 10

La Tere Smelled of Fish 13

Balloons 15

A Boy's Life: Six Episodes 17

Soliloquio Tijua 19

One Moment Saves a Day 21

Prima 22

The Fever of Being 25

Some Joke 27

III. CEREMONY

Lo 31

Man's Fate 32

Houston to San Antone w/ Convicts 33

San Antonio Bus Terminal, Feb. 21, 1985: Midnight 35

Meadowlark: Two Songs 37

June 8 40

Listen, He Said 41

Sombra 43

Midnight Lamp 44

Migration 48

Ring of Fire 49

The Bones of A Small Fire 51

IV. HORSES

Horses 55

V. FINAL CONVOCATION

And the Wind to Blow Us On 77

Here's the Dream 82

For César and Bette González:
in loco parentis.

How lost life's been. Afraid of waking up.
So afraid to take the dream.

Fields of the Nephilim

I
First Convocation

The Sunday Drive

1965

They never touched.   Not a hand,
not a brush of thigh, not
a fingernail clacked over their bowl
of Fritos as they watched
the nightly Vietnam report.
One glass of sherry
a night.

She had a horror of his flesh.
In his flesh she saw all flesh.
He lumbered up the hall
unclothed, his flesh wooden
and unsheathed.
        He drove her like a storm
scattered into her back room
as far from him as she could sleep.
Wedding rings long locked
in sewing boxes not forgotten.

And in this house a frightened son
who ate and ate and ate.

Still, some Sundays
sun would break the winter clouds.
In place of church
they had the scratchy seats of a '49 Ford
that shamed her so she'd claim
it was a '52.

He and she
in the front seat, smoking.   Sophisticated
chatter: Ian Fleming, Jackie Gleason, Scott Fitzgerald.
The son in the back with his plastic guns.
Green soldiers.
Thinking, it's all right this time.
This time it's all right.
This time we might drive
all around the world!

But his father's hidden need
drove him to it,
he needled her
in his wheedling
sensitive
disappointed
accent.

He called her unkind, cruel, a vindictive bitch
who said the wrong things at the wrong times to the wrong people.
And she said
> *You fucking Mexican!*

Ah, you see, he said
to the son, what your mother is really like.
As though appalled, the car pulled to the curb
and hung there, panting.
He turned his smile to her,
his pink-faced raging tender wounded victim's smile.
Do you see now, boy? Do you see your high-class American
mother?

So they went back home.
She slammed out of the car and flung
herself into her lonely bed.
He began to whistle, lit a Pall Mall,
backed out, sped to a bowling alley
where he took a waitress from behind on antiseptic tiles.
Sunday spilled away like salt.

As for me, I carried my soldiers to the back yard.
Then, after a little while, it got dark.
Only this night was quieter than usual.
I crawled under the bushes with the cats.
Snails made small scrapings on the leaves.
The silence that was neither Spanish
nor English
was my prayer.
And God was good:
there came no sound until morning.

II
Procession

I Tried to Write A Poem About This
Once A Year for Thirteen Years.

I tried to enter the car—
my father driving, interior dim in late desert night,
lit by the dash, by the pumping radio:
rancheras beat across Chihuahua's haunted heat.
How my little cousin Melba smelled of hair and
flesh, how my aunt drowsed and my uncle and father
murmured in the front seat, manly mysteries I
stayed awake for: cojones, cigarettes, bulls,
menudo. How late it was. How my father
drove for twenty hours.

To show the dark of the dunes
before us, vague in moonlight: how
blue-red lightning flashed in the distance,
so subtle at first that you couldn't tell
if they were there or your eyes
were throwing nerve-sparks from no sleep.
It took a minute to see
the bolts were on the ground.
How I said, "Look out, Papa."
How he slowed down, and how I felt
so powerful at that instant: the words
I spoke could pull the eternal machine
of my father back from his speed.

How slow we came
around the bend,
and what we saw.
I always tried
to show the glass,
the liquids spread
that threw back light:
oil, glass, and blood.

Men ran the far side of the road,
frantic flashlights probed among desert trees:
mesquite, palo verde, ocotillo.
"What is this," my father said. And my uncle,
muy Mexicano, ordered my aunt
to hide Melba's head beneath her arm, to look
into her hair.

And the solid wall of metal and meat
before us: the split-
level passenger bus
welded head-on to the semi.
Twelve-wheeled, eight-
wheel drive, dead
still sticking.
The shoes of the bus driver hanging from the upraised tomb
of the dashboard.
The colorful fleshy garlands
looping from the windows like
the party was about to begin.
The engine of the bus
knocked out the back, lying
silent behind.
Smoke. Odd mounds
scattered, indistinct
in the flash flash flashing.

And the smaller details that never wanted to fit:
the one cop swinging a lantern alone.
How he begged us to get out of there.
How he said: "They passed on the curve."
And: "Seventy, eighty miles an hour."
And: "They're searching the trees for a baby
        that flew out the window."
And how we drove on through the night,
there was nothing between us
but the radio,
the tally as it was counted, bland voices
bouncing across black lands. 100 miles
from any city.
One ambulance
at each end
of the highway.

And how we'd hear it coming four miles away,
watch it hurtle, recede, return.
And I could never quite capture the school girls.
On a trip into Mexico, coming home, fifteen,
twenty school girls. All my age.
And you could see them in their uniforms
holding hands. They stood in rough circle
out among the cactus, gray as ash

in the half light.
They were singing—a hymn, the national
anthem, the school song, I don't know.
All these voices tiny as ghosts
bounced off the metal.
Singing and singing.
Every voice
as we left
stolen by the wind.

Abelino Garcia:
A Song of My Elder

he watches angels bleed
up pinetree saplings, rise
through knotty trunks and spring
at dawn's fragmented light

>   *nos hace falta un emiliano zapata*

he reads the roadmaps of heaven
in the chip of light
in raven's eye

across the ladybug's domed back
the universe revealed:
red and curved
and halved—

he sops up turpentine
sweat in a faded bandanna,
perfumes himself
with the fluttered smell
of grape vines, vino,
olives, maize

old pearl diver who swam
north across the desert

>   *nomás nos faltan las plumas*
>   *pa' ser puro indio*

when thunderheads hear and heed
his word, rush up the coast
thick with dust, pitch
electric fits

he sews the falling shadows
of his homeland
to his hat
with drumming threads
of rain

>   *esta lluvia me sabe a la paz*

women come to him with ills:
he fills with herbs, with wine

their puckered navels,
fumes the dolors from their veins:

forges teas that frighten
tapeworms from the gut:
he binds thick black-lined ankles
tight in roots: they pulse
their smell into the blood,
unfreeze the knees of men
who stay for supper

> *pancho villa era un cabrón*
> *pero nunca lo doblaron*

he pulls his dentures free
to spit into the weeds.
he has adobe palms

and then
another magic:

the white man's tubes
screw up his nose
so suddenly: pump air
into his sparking brain
where black fires light

his wooden legs nailed to a bed:
the one man never meant
to greet a sunrise on his back:
his eyes are hammered flat

I watch him
turn to desert sand,
his color bleeds
up IV saplines
from a nipple in his hand

> *usted me dirá "usted"*
> *porque así un hombre muestra*
> *el respeto*

Abelino wings with brother crow
over memory's floodplain
bedpan unattended
his silent song concealed
beneath the edge of a sheet

he will not look at me,
demands
a wordless leaving,
angry sleep,
because *los sonsabichis* doctors
won't give him back his teeth.

La Tere Smelled of Fish

Day shift's closing bells
stilled conveyer belts: La Tere
and the other women
stepped away from eighteen-
year-old bald spots worn
into the factory floor,

the two million razor-toothed lids
a day stilled in their sure flight
above hungry cans—a constellation
of tin moons:

fish-gutters
sluiced blood
from rubber legs,
propped long knives
in wooden slots, hung
slick aprons limp
as strangled crows
beside them:

then the buses home, white
nurse-dresses pink at the hem
with blood, black
hair oiled dull and caught
tight to heads with fishnet,
scent of albacore, yellowtail, strong
as illness all around them—
they divided in the Four Directions:
San Ysidro, Chula Vista,
National City, Barrio Logan:

La Tere came home and picked
opal scales
from her calves
from her legs
from her shoes:

her back bent down
and couldn't come up,
shoulderblades dead fins

from the canning angle
of her days.

One eye sliding loose
and nobody knew why.
She went to bed at eight
and heard the seashore roar
of silver machines.

Up at four, silent
in the silent rooms, three
tortillas with butter, a little tuna:
then she went alone
into the fish-belly dawn,
and when one day she didn't come back
from Starkist, they sealed her house
like a can.

That was the summer of '59,
the summer of '65,
the summer of '71.
That was the summer
of her life.

Balloons

You
knew Tijuana's hills. I
was new

to the dirt mystery
of those streets. The steep
arroyos.

You
knelt behind la
casa. You

called the meat
hamburguesa, ground beef
10 cents

for a pound. I
looked up at you, handsome, up
to you,

you were black
against the sun.
You

knew karate, you
had rifles
that blew pigeons'

heads to gray
feather spray,
you

tipped the metal jar
and filled
balloons. I

laughed
beside you,
wrapped

the meat
around the red
(always red)

balloons.
Then we
two

went from yard to yard
and fed
the dogs.

You whispered these secrets
to me.
And I

closed my eyes. I
pried up the lid,
ignored the sting,

tasted the bitter
burned almonds
of manhood.

A Boy's Life:
Six Episodes

I.

I was born in flame.   The Mexicans wheeled my mother, belly-up, belly aimed at a fingernail moon, into a room upstairs five miles from the racetrack on the escape route east of Tijuana.   And there, set scalpels afire.   They cut me out with smoking knives.   My father boasted I was born

II.

with an erection.   Hiding in Tijuana's dogshit basement, sick old sheep-dog spewing across walls.   My cousin's black deep room, and mounds of moldering pornographic secrets.   Black widows above my head, red hourglass guts and pinheads armed with poisoned needles.   Smeared, in black and white, women on floors, barstools, beds, slack-lipped, their tired skin gone white in the camera glare

III.

as snow in Durango.   The highest peaks above the pine-top waterfalls. All the road the loveliest girl in the car ahead hung her face out the window and vomited.   A baby goat locked in our trunk battered his head against the metal and cried.   When we stopped, starving dogs licked the girl's breakfast from the door.   It was the same color as the wildflowers.   Then men pressed a pistol into my hand and led me to the river bank.   And I braced my hand and tried to take

IV.

aimless, the wind carried the dust from behind our house.   A family of tubercular children spilled what they'd brought up of their lungs into battered steel cups.   Then dumped their red cough into the dirt.   The dirt that blew to me, and brought strange spores into my lungs, that clotted my dreams with choking, pared me down like a sliver of wood carved by

V.

his knife, at the back of my neck, felt as tender sweeping by as a summer breeze lifting a lover's

VI.

hair.   Lying in the arms of a brown woman not my mother, in the sweat
that clouded in that crook, I was small as canaries caged on the porch.
A brown-black nipple against my cheek, universal vastness of a cushioned
breast pressed along the curve of my thumbnail skull, my rugged wet
cough in the stark cage of my ribs, my eyes large as shells washed up
with a drop of sky trapped in each, and her small cross dangling gold
in the folds of her dress.   It was black hair.   My starfish hands reached
for that midnight silk, as if the dark could feed me.   As if the hired
comfort of a stranger gave me life.   As if the insistent color of nothing
were all I'd ever know of milk.

Soliloquio Tijua

Me levanto
pa las 4 y
media cada
día, bien
tempranito

es cuando el aigre
stá todo fresco y
no jiede al sol y
a los perros y los
tractores y el mal
aliento del humo.

las moscas stan pegadas a la pader
y casi no se ven en la oscuridad . . .
dormiditas como mi vieja tirada en
la esquina, negra y flaca, piernas
abiertas y su olor pesado bajo las
cobijas—roncando y dando patadas.
ella sueña mucho, sueña de mares
que se la llevan gritando.   pobrecita
mi mujer—le levanto el bestido y
le dejo mis humos metidos adentro.

entonces me salgo pafuera, detras del cantoncito
onde tengo el pozo y no sé lo que tengo, pero mi
cuerpo suelta chorros de pintura y me arde—pos
ya sabes que el mismo chile que te pica la boca
te pica el culo tambien y así es la vida, qué no.

mi vieja ya se despierta, y le stá metiendo papeles y mierda seca
al hornito pa prender el fuego y me calienta el café y los huevos
que me robé del pollo de la manuela—y los frijoles son de esos
misioneros gringos.   ah, y si no estoy crudo, le levanto la falda
y le agarro las nalgas de mi vieja, que son cafes y duras, mangos
cubiertos con aceite, mis humos saliendo y corriendole los muslos
como corriente pequeña de leche saltandose por un arroyo suave.

pero cuando ando crudo, no
tengo ganas de hacer nada,
y no me gusta ni hablarle,

viejo, me dice mi vieja—
traes cara de pendejo. es
que soy pendejo, le digo.
es que la vida stá bien
cabrona, le digo. es que
cuando ando crudote, creo
que puedo ver lo que me
queda: dolor de cabeza,

olor de mujer,
y dias de noche,
y noches oscuras,
y un viaje tan
largo que nunca
regresamos. y yo
me iré sin que-
rer. yo quien
nunca me he
podido salir
del desgra-
ciado dompe.

One Moment Saves a Day

like this:
two goofy Chicano boys
baseball caps backwards
on their heads, # 41 bus. &
1 gets off. The other
says to him: "You
        study hard!"

The sun ignites.
I can see
all across the city:
far sage, like gray buttons
sews itself to the hem
of the mountains.

Prima

Prima,
ni siquiera se tu nombre,
tu padre me cargó en sus brazos
de la clínica donde nací
a la casa de nuestra abuelita
que crecía como un hongo amarillo
en la orilla
de un arroyo
en las alturas de Tijuana.

Aquí te lo cuento
por primera vez.

Tu padre era el hermano mayor
de mi papá,
y en esos dias
(les gustaba decir *en aquel entonces*)
todavia eran
jovenes, fuertes,
vivos.

Tu padre me cargó en sus brazos
mientras tú
estabas saliendo
del dolor oscuro
de tu madre
en algun rincón desconocido,
algun callejón Mexicano
sin saber que no tenias futuro,
que para tí
tu padre siempre
sería un misterio.

El
se fue con su propia familia,
cumpliendo con sus responsabilidades.
Un hombre
decente.

Crecímos, Prima.
Y un día entre tantos,
vino tu madre a la casa amarilla.

Era chaparra, prietita,
otra María con rebozo,
chorreada.
Decían
    gente pelada.

Tú estabas con ella.
No jugamos.

Yo era el hijo preferido,
el güerito,
ojos azules.
Y tú . . .
pues imagínate.
    Fea
decían.
    India la pobrecita.
Tenías granos en las piernas.
Llorabas
dijeron
de atiro.

Nuestra abuelita
con su buena educación
les dió algo de comer
y te corrió
        delicadamente
de la casa.
A la calle.
Pa'fuera.
Pa'bajo.
Al Río
de Tijuana, a
un cuarto de cartón
en "Cartolandia."
Y en pocos años
ese río
se llevó todas
de las Indias
en un diluvio
de tractores.
Desaparecidas.
Limpiadas
todas juntas
de la memoria.

Te fuiste.

Y ahora, Prima,
tu existencia se explica—
si es que admitimos
que existes—
con una sonrisita
socarrona.
—Pues, tú sabes cómo son los hombres.
—Es que esas viejas prietas
  se enloquecen con los varones
  guapos.
—Es que esas Marías cabronas
  siempre andan embarazadas.

Te sueño.
Oigo tus pasos
en las calles
y volteo, rápido
pero no te encuentro.

Te vine a decir una cosa:
tu padre murió
ya hace mucho tiempo.
Nuestra abuelita lo abandonó tambien,
diciendo que no aguantaba el dolor
último de su rey.
Tienes hermanos.
Despadrezados.
Tu abuela se hizo tonta
y murió pequeña,
borrada.
Y yo, aquí,
con mis palabritas.

Prima,
tu padre murió,
dijeron,
llorando
de atiro.

Se fue gritando por su madre
como tú te fuiste ese día
chillando por tu papá.

The Fever of Being

Perhaps
I caught it in Durango.
In Durango
orange rocks and black
where I drank the waterfalls
I drank the raw waterfalls of Durango
I licked the water green as leaves from the rocks
scooped the water from the dark volcanic folds
swallowed shadows of bulls that stood
in pinetop cataracts on weeping peaks
of Durango.
I was on my knees,
pushed my face through the lace
of the falls, of the ferns, put my lips to the stone
bit off hunks of water, and the gold dust
and the water-spiders, and the fish bones
and the threads unstrung
from women's clothes,
and the bright amoebas clenched
around the spores
poured in my fever's mouth,
laid roots in all the silt
I'd gulped in mountain chill
of high Durango.
Or was it Culiacán and the heat,
burning earth where poppies
pop bright colorbursts
where helicopter gunships raid the fields
where peasant heroin harvesters shot from the dams
turn in water pink behind the wall that cracks
that moans
above the city.
Crickets fondle buildings
brushy-legged, they sound like rusted hinges
pulling free
the whole place
swinging wide
all night . . .

all night . . .
all night . . .
all
night
. . .
.

Some Joke

Some joke unexplained
blew pale smoke of skin
over my brown bones: some
joke took my vision, black,
opened it for sky-bright eyes.

My pink tongue
forever seeks sweet
brown nipple of heartwords:
my dark seed unseen
in white tide.

I would walk cool rows
of crow-haunted corn,
hear nothing but the hiss
of colorless wind,
green leaf blades cutting
my ties, God's
dry lips
breathing on the honeyed plains.
I would push beyond sight,
into green
shadowed earth,
dig a silent place
where sun would never find me:
my hair
the same color
as the corn.

III
Ceremony

Lo

Lo
ve
is
li
ke
se
tt
in
gy
ou
rs
el
fo
nf
ir
ea
nd
ho
pi
ng
yo
ud
on
't
ge
tb
ur
ne
d.

Man's Fate

And then one day
you get up
and she's gone.
And the burns on the pots
remind you. And her forgotten
cream underpants in the dreamdust
under the bed remind you. And the seat
of the toilet indicts you. And the noise
of the silence infects you.
You try every remedy
your man's small mind can conjure:
call old lovers. Naked all day. Crap
with the door open.
Defiant beer.

And the creak of your knees when you pray again
reminds you. And the babyblue box
of homeless tampons reminds you.
And the Christmas tinsel stuck
to the back of the bookshelf reminds you.
And the dip in the mattress,
the hair in the brush,
the three year old
flower of blood
on the sheet,
and the day,
the light,
the sun,
the night, the hours, the minutes, the years
conspire to remind and remind
and remind you.

Houston to San Antone
w/ Convicts

All 6 of them just-out, blinking
at the big world like kittens: Chicanos
w/ blue Bic tattoos, cholo watch-caps
pulled down on cellblock haircuts.
Bus pilot could smell 7 years
of the joint's dust on them.
Suspicious as a night guard
doing head-count, he dropped
an arm across the doorway.
"You drunk?" he said.
"Nossir."
"Been doing drugs?"
"Nossir."

They were drunk.
Everybody on the bus
including the driver
would be drunk too.

"Going home, sir."
"Don't give me no trouble."
"No *suh!*"
"I ain't in no mood
to put up with no trouble."
"No *suh!*"

"All right, then."
He climbed on, shades
sharp as a cop's, and he nodded
at us, curt: In Control
of The Situation.
Timid now
as hummingbirds
the vatos
collided and tripped
to the back of the bus.

They sighed like the air brakes
when we peeled away
from Houston.

Scrub smoked by us in the night
all the way to Seguín
every tree a puff
from God's forgotten cigarette.
The bus was full of snoring—sailors
and drifters sleeping, legs
like fences in the aisle.
Except the 6 in back, unasleep, watchful.
They murmured over their cards, voices
somber as the Mass: *Gloria, Gloria, Gloria.*
Fists clenched
around the red eyes
of their Lucky Strikes.

At a station
no bigger than an exercise yard
they walked
melancholy circles.

San Antonio showed itself,
looked airborne, some vast backlit
mother-ship, ethereal & pure.
Each of our windows
must have looked like fish tanks
from the street: the 6 in back
crowded w/ eager faces, breath
fogging hearts
before their lips.
But the station, almost midnight,
flanked by police cars, dark
in the mysterious street, pointed at us.

Everybody woke up.
Some of us laughed.
6 dreadful voices
rolling up the aisle

crying:
    OH!

crying:
    NO!

The driver turned the wheel
like he was letting go the gas.

San Antonio Bus Terminal, Feb. 21, 1985: Midnight

Waiting for Nephtalí de Leon.
It's late.
A guy in a black mesh body-shirt
says: "Where you goin?"
"Right here," I say.
"Here," he says.
"What's there
here?"

The video game in the corner is talking.
I've been listening to it for half an hour.
It's saying: "Super basketball.
Substitute.   Here we go.
Oop!
Jump-shot.
Substitute.   Here we go.
Oop!
Jump-shot.
Super basketball.
Substitute.   Here we go."

Black Mesh says: "I'm goin to Ol' Messico."
"*Really*," I say.
He works the gimme cap on his head
like a pump-handle, filling his head
with insights.
He steps up to the machine, plugs in
a coin. "Here we go," it says.

I sip vending-machine coffee to stay awake.
Boys in the street
cruise sailors, signs read: ROOMS
$6.00. Everything tilts.
He misses every shot.
"Bastard!" he says, hits the machine
like he's knocking out
its teeth.

&: "I quit!"
He walks in a circle.
&: "I give up!"

He swoops back at it.
Walks away.

It must be the hour, or the coffee,
but as he walks away, the machine
says: "Shut up, Scott. Oop! Shut up,
Scott.
Oop!
Scott?
Shut up."

Meadowlark: Two Songs

1.

Carrie's singing again,
    crazy old Black woman, well
        of course she's crazy, every

body in Meadowlark's crazy
    or old. But Carrie's
        the craziest of the flock

in her chair, gospel-singing
    her hallucinations,
        testifying

yellow palms uplifted
    two last fangs yellower
        than her palms, her song

endless. "Oh Lord. Woe Lord."
    "Shut up," her roommates say,
        "Why don't you

shut the goddamn hell up."
    But Carrie's singing,
        eyes to heaven, *Woe Lord,*

tied to her chair, tied
    in her piss, *Oh Lord.*
        The one time she

shut up, she looked me
    full in the face and cried
        "Louis! Get them chickens

out of there! Boy!
    Said get the chickens! Water's
        coming up!" Then

her eyes cut to the door
    tears steady as Old Miss
        and watched her Louis

go forever down the flood.
    Oh Lord.
        Woe Lord.

2.

Meadowlark of steel nests,
    beds side-raised to hold
        hatchling dreams of flight,

nightmare kicks.
    Arms like wings, some soldier's
        grandmother whose name

fell out upon her pillow
    last Christmas eve and rolled
        off the edge and shattered

to dust, drifts. All smiles.
    Naked as a baby bird.
        As wrinkled. Pink

All down her cross-hatched back,
    bare belly marked by crows
        who must have walked her

like a snowbank: red
    Y marks cut across
        caesarean scars. Slack

navel like a baby's mouth
    pulled down in sorrow, crying
        to be kissed.

Chin whiskers white
    and hard as nesting twigs,
        her ancient sex

a whisk of fading smoke.
    She coos to me, coming
        forward, ever forward,

presses my hands
    to her empty envelopes
        tender as fog

and nurses lead her off.
    "I love you," she says. "How
        I do love you. Love

me, please." Her feet
    make lip-smack sounds
        as she's led away.

They tie her to a bed.
    "I love you," she says.
        "You beautiful man."

Her cracked lips
    gasp apart: air
        moves into her

then withdraws.
    Her lover of dust
        falling back across the sky.

June 8

97 degrees, 80% humidity
10:40 at the Mug'N'Muffin.
Up all night.
Today this woman went by me
in Harvard Square
wearing a pantsuit made entirely
of trash bags. The dark green kind.
I almost passed out
just watching.
People turned around to stare at her.
She rippled like the Charles River.
There must have been steam escaping her,
clouds collecting under her arms,
a fog bank rolling up from her thighs.
Her whole body might have been whistling.
She could have melted right there—
run out through the cuffs of her plastic pants,
people slipping on her
and falling down in the street.
But she didn't. She kept walking.
And everybody turned back to their papers
and iced coffees, thinking
I am on a strange journey,
and where I'm going
I don't want to know.

Listen, He Said

I was working in an all-nighter
selling beer and cigarettes on a hill
above Interstate 5.

One morning before dawn
a handsome young man
tall as Davy Crockett
came in for beer:

hair to his shoulders
unbuttoned work-shirt
Marlboros in the pocket
no hair on his muscled chest
dark nipples.

Two gleaming mechanical arms
extended from his elbow stumps
like chromed construction cranes
bright pincers at the ends: I watched
him clip his hand to the neck
of a bottle of Bud.

"Hi," he said.

"Hey," I said.

"How's it going?" I said.

"Fine," he said.

I was hypnotized by his gleam.

"Listen," he said

"I got a bunch of change
in my pocket, but
I can't get at it with
these."

He opened one pincer
at eye level
peeked
between the hooks.

"So," he said,
hooking one pocket
open

"could you get it out?"

"Go on," he said.

"Reach in there.

It's okay.

Just put your hand right
in there."

My fingers in his tight pocket, then,
digging through lint for his dimes
his warm quarters.   Beer
on his breath.

"Yeah," he said.

"There you go," he said.

I was stretched across the counter
and the cold metal against my wrist.

I pulled out 50 cents.

"That do it?" he said.

"Sure," I said.   "Why not."

"Which way's north?" he said.

I pointed.   With my whole hand.
My entire arm.

"You headed that way?" I said.

"Thumbing a ride," he said.

"Oh," I said.

"See ya," he said
waving metal.

The aluminum doors moved together behind him.
Outside, the palest fog came in and covered everything.

Sombra

La poesía es la sombra de la memoria.

—José Emilio Pacheco

Mi cara
en la orilla
de tu pelvis

Yo
hincado
a tus pies:
suplicante
alabando

a tu olor
de mar, mariposa,
margarita

Un minuto, no más

Tú, ahora
tan delgada en mi memoria
como estas telarañas
de tinta

lupita

Midnight Lamp

Can you hear me calling you.

     Awake too long.
These graveyard nights.   These sleepless hours.
These spitting lights.   The stars outside
are salt: they burn

my eyes.   Inside, I hide.
The shift I work turns skin to gauze
so thin the feathers in my soul blow through
and drift the store.   The midnight hookers kick
them out the door:
Carla's in her cowboy hat again; Ginger brings her
seventh sailor in for beer.
     I sweep my dreams down aisle six.

     These disinfected sighs.
Scorpions climb from the canyons.   I find them
on the magazines, the pinball machine.   They reach for me,
track me, strain to sting my shadow.
They carry the tears of the dead in their tails.

       This forgotten earring
    laying on the floor / Facing coldly
      towards the door.
Bowling alley moon rolls over the roof.   Other people sleep
in tender beds.   Their nightmares run on eight cold legs.
I pull them from the windows, carry them in pails
drowned in Lysol.

This wall of papered glass.

II.

       These last few nights, the dancer comes
at three a.m. She drives
another man's car into the lot. I lock
down the machines, leave
the empty skull-white room
to hum alone.

Inside, beside
her. I smell her perfume, the meadows
of her sweat. Overwhelmed by hair.

I take her feet in my lap,
slip my hands under her skirt,
work the muscles in her thighs.
She loves the owner of the car.
She cries.

III.

     This lonely man.
He comes at dawn, always
before the sun. We watch him
push the doors. I run inside.
     This neon sky.

His glasses carry fingerprints on either lens,
like someone tried to steal his sight
and dropped it.
He buys a dozen paperbacks:
The Butcher, The Executioner, Conan.
The light tubes make dark arcs
beneath his breasts.
I see her out there.
He buys:
     Yoo-Hoo, Slimjims,
     cupcakes, Mars Bars.
His blush, his sweaty smile: Don't laugh at me.
     Pepsi, ice cream,
     corn chips, bean dip,
     peanuts.
Her engine starts.
Her brake lights flare.
Come on come on come on.
He fumbles, drops
his money:
change
is everywhere. He says
"It really doesn't
doesn't bother me
too much at all."

She pulls away.

I watch her go.

She's gone.

IV.

It's just the ever-
falling dust that makes it so hard
for me to see.
Outside, I wait for sun.
The fat man goes alone.
I sweep cigarettes
off the sand.
The stars have crumbled, powdered
down across the canyon.   I watch the chill
wind pull the moon's plug—all across the hill
feathers eddy.

Engines
on the interstate
serenade the dancer home.

Can you hear me calling you?

This is the soul-mine.
I'm going down
          down
          down.

for the dancer

Migration

The subway rose from under Boston's skirts,
turned into a trolley, rolled west
through tenement woods:
chestnut hills, then backs
of laundry-draped buildings:
five family slanted porches, then
golf courses.

Deer eating behind
dead Chevies.

To a job I hated, a job of gray-faced
gray-haired gray-suited men.

It was always winter. Even in August
the river was crusty all around its lips
with freeze. Icicles
drooled from rainspouts. I'd nod
at my cancer-eaten superiors
who didn't know they were dying,
all of us standing, 7:00 a.m.,
waiting in the lot by the trainyard
for the company van to pick us up,
haul us away.

Greyhound buses swung in for a 5
minute stop before hitting the pike,
exotic names tattooed on their brows:
Worcester, Albany, Cleveland, Phila PA,
Atlantic City, Wheeling, Detroit, Atlanta.
All marvelous places! Where I was not.

The sky, a flat gray lid of ice
And the Canada geese came over.
Big leaders at the head of each flying wedge.
Their rusty *sqwonks* the only sound for miles.
Working at the oars of the sky.
The dark magnets in their heads
not only pulling them
away but telling them
        exactly
how to get there.

Ring of Fire

Ring around shimmered ring
of burned and rock-churned light:
Anza's hurt and hammered floor,
great Painted Desert hangs unframed,
bright in the gallery of night

O Jericho, your ancient voices sing
hosannas to the brilliant King
who gleams high over Sinai:
whose blinding waves splash back
from stone to stone and waver
swaying bushes, rippling
up the winding ways of Zion

O Chihuahua, Villa slings
his rifle on his back and rides
black motorcycle up your spine,
strides hollow, dark with pride
to drink your sun like cactus wine.   Sidewinders
swirl the tideless beach: scorpions
trail cold tails down talus slopes
to plow thin furrow-rows as fine
as lines across my palm—
a field of dust that devils
tall in wind to dance, tornado-hipped
and pale: it slips across your lava, sand, your shale:
it thrusts itself up canyons out of reach

O ring of fire, hard and clean-
est point where planet spins,
charred free of lies, where black wings fly
slack thermals searching bones
of those few sinners, outlaws, saints
who went alone into your blaze,
who'd always known that in your face
the truth begins—unholy plain,
you make us sacred: your silence slays restraint
and timid human song takes claim of us: tides of blood
chime in veins: the climbing thrum of thongs
that strum our lungs and legs: the heart's

faint hum: our dumb-struck tongues
sing glory in disguise: we sigh—
all equal here, all small before your heat
that flares uncaring, ceaseless, fair and focused
as a rattler's quartz-chip eye, bared
and tracking, stony,
bored and blasted dry:
your stare is honed,
and seeing everything,
is blind.

The Bones of A Small Fire

a love that rushes by without handles

—Jay Griswold

At the tail-end of summer, under the nose
of the Old Man in the Mountain,
in the misty breath of autumn
rolled down New Hampshire's valleys
on its way to certain snow,
beside lakes small as quarters
burning with ridiculous
maple colors, my woman & I

on our fall into personal
ice-storms, just about dead
but not yet sure if we needed
burial, if only someone could crack
loose enough granite from
frozen soil, drop us in to hibernate
for eternity in that permafrost
of disaster,

we huddled at a small fire, ghostly
clouds exhausted by Mt. Washington
crawled from tree to tree, eating stars,
a raven's cough, a porcupine's mewl
muffled to a giggle
as if some melancholy angel had dropped,
old voices around us in the ferns
and we, barely able

to look into each other's eyes, bled
so much for so long, no more blood
could come: small stones tumbled
from our veins: fungus
in lightning-gutted pines
glowed like Neruda's last gasp: I
was learning the architecture of the blues:
she had risen in the ghost dance.

Our tent was wet as skin
on a knife blade. Our fire's bones
fine as needles, sewed the dark
to our eyelids. My God, everywhere

51

night.   And we
had forgotten how to pray.
She lay another twig in the flame.
For an instant of mercy, we were warm.

Everyone I have ever loved is gone.

IV

Horses

HORSES

—for Jay Griswold

when the hand falls apart it makes
a handful of bones
                    —A.R. Ammons

Ride the highway West
Baby . . .

I.

When the land falls apart it leaves
a handful of bones.

I slept on a Utah shore
while lightning storms swarmed around
the buttes / their fire legs
touched down across the gorge
          exploded trees.
Below, the water
lay as dead
as a bison's tongue.

Down there, drowned
Linwood town
drifted with limp snapshots,
choked on silt.
A table cloth adrift
looked like a ghost
at midnight.

The view from under
Linwood's bone-white cottonwoods
—murky. Storm flashes
pulsed gray and faint
above.

Largemouth bass
swam long-dead balustrades:

their shapely lips took in
the exoskeletons
of memories.

Today, the only way you get to town
is dive: bubbles of your last breath
combing through your hair: you
drown in Linwood Square, grab
hold of the flagpole and pull
yourself down / join
your private ghosts who wait
who stroll the muddy lane
linked fingers
in the cold.

Dead horses hitched
to wagons full of sighs.

II.

I rode a horse West
for 500 years.
I met Sherman Alexie
in the Uinta mountains.
He said: Have you seen
Jay Griswold?
I said: He rode his horse
to the moon.
He said: Linda Hogan
has met fifteen white boys
who all think
they're reincarnated
Crazy Horse.
I said: They buried Tom Horn
at the end of my block,
and nobody thinks
they're him.

He said: I came all this way
and I don't know the language—
this whole tribe speaks
in whispers.
I said: These are the mountains
that run east and west,
the only ridgeline
you can ride
to the land of the dead.
He said: Is Tom Horn here?
I said: They say Tom Horn lies restless—holds
1,000 bullets
in his mouth.
He said: It's hard work
being dead.
I said: Sherman,
that horse you're on
is made of bones.
He said: At least
he don't
eat much.

III.

You probably went there.
Utah's sere lip, scraping all the flavor
off Flaming Gorge, this little tent
so piss-poor in the rain I had to stretch
canvas over the roof so I could sleep dry.
Right where gradually thickening water
buried the town, once half-lively
(anyway as lively as a town in Utah gets)
with cross-streets, elms, thirty-nine
cottonwoods, and a post office.
A truck came to dig up the graves, cart off heirlooms and bikes,
but nobody could winch the sweat-stains out of the beds:
Cats the color of Orange Crush tried
for seven weeks to pry the shadows of lovers
from the bedroom foundations, and old Doctor Williams's
chaw-spit stain in the shape of an eagle
refused to leave the crackling driveway
of the Esso station.   What the hell, it hadn't pumped
a pint of gas in twenty years.

The West . . . is the best.

The distant sluice-gates closed.   You know this one,
they've been telling it for years around Glen Canyon,
neon trout sunk in sludge
back-filling, silent as stinking gray snow.   Rabbits flooded
in the den, the last kit fox on the last bobbing branch
going under, gentle as a French kiss.

Water came creeping.   Up steps.   All the ghosts
raised their bony feet and fretted.   On up
the flow: window-boxes surrendered,
turds in the stables took off like meteors,
forgotten stamps in the P.O. licked
themselves to shelves and widened to mush.
Each roof, for one half day, was a perfect wedged island.
Baffled crows perched there, saying *What?*
Say what?

IV.

I picked up a book
at the side of Tom Horn's grave
and this is what it said:

> On the morning of November 20, 1903, Horn walked up the steps of the gallows erected in the jail's courtyard. He smiled as his friends Charlie and Frank Irwin sang, at his request, "Life's Railway to Heaven," the words of the maudlin ballad echoing in the barren chamber:

> > Life is like a mountain railroad,
> > With an engineer that's brave;
> > We must make the run successful,
> > From the cradle to the grave;
> > Watch the curves, the fills, the tunnels,
> > Never falter, never quail;
> > Keep your hand upon the throttle, and your eye
> > upon the rail.

> In the sudden silence after the last note had died away, Charlie called out: "Be game."
> Horn nodded. "You bet I will," he replied in a firm voice.
> Then he helped Undersheriff Richard Proctor adjust the noose and black cap. His last words were to County Clerk Joseph Cahill, who helped him to the trap door.
> "Ain't losin' your nerve, are you, Joe?"

—James D. Horan

V.

I go to
nature because man is scary

A.R. Ammons
said that: I have stolen it.

When the words
look good, I put my gun
to their heads and back slowly
out the door: I whisper: *smile.*

VI.

Got a letter from Tom Horn today.
In it he enclosed
a glass plate photograph—
it cracked, like lightning
across his face
        but still
you could see
he was
a curious man.

And here is the picture,

and here is what he wrote:

Behold : Myself.

The West is the best.

Once you're dead, they don't let you kill.
And I'm an exterminating son of a bitch.

I lie still in Arapaho soil,
but my bones remember restless days
the creak of saddles

and the scent of oil
rainbow blue on the barrel
of the Sharp's, hindsights
raised and focused.

Flatiron mountains unseen at my head,
a headstone better
than Billy the Kid
ever got.

Friends,
I reflect
upon the migration of fate,
that brought me to life
with a gift for killing.
Had God's own grasp
of dying and living:
I could deal the end
as clean and crisp
as a peregrine's beak
that frees a pigeon
from its breath.

I ran
the prairies
and did
what I did.
What was given
to me to do.
And I earned a dollar
doing it.

Now this.
A man could starve for dying.

Grass
pulls my hair
into its roots.
My trigger finger
stings
like ants in my bones
to curl and fire—
my soul connected
to the bullet, bright
trajectory at a thousand miles
a minute,

whistling
a silver wind: a hornet's flight
300 yards through buffalo grass
windage bearing
slight askew,
the droop
of its flight
red-hot mirror
of earth's
curve

faster than the sound
of itself:
the target looming quick and
tall, taller
than the Black Hills.
The bullet
hits.

My breath
cracks the spine,
sprouts the bloom
red petals in an instant
then blows
the candle flame
to smoke.

And he falls
as he hears the *bang*
catch up.
In his mind,
the loveliest scenes
of childhood walnut fudge,
parasols, the sweet scent
of his mother's breasts.
No pain at all.   It's like
a waking dream.

And on his lips,
as if a prayer,
my name.

VII.

In the streambed, the stallion screams. His eyes weep a crust, blood lays red cracks through his vision. Mane catches fire: small sparks roll from the ends of the hair, fling about him like droplets. Hooves hit the rock: lava seeps, steam rising all around him.

The mares turn as one, splash away laughing and fretting among themselves. They pucker with his scent, their tails rise and their smoke clouds the entire day. Comanches read the smoke columns from a distance.

The stallion rears, bucks, bites chunks out of the clouds with deadly flat yellow teeth.

The mares awaken in their bellies. Ghost horses within kick their feet. Push at their ribs. Wombs swing wide their gates, the floors slick with blood and delicious dripping forage.

And he comes. Squirts of barbed wire fly from his loins, trap ten acre prairie plots. Coyotes strangle in the wires; the buffalo stops and stares stupidly, not understanding his passion. The stallion runs five hundred miles, his eyes rolling out of his head, brown stones with holes drilled through. Wide wakes of fire spread behind him, swing open and eat the tall grass, the homesteads, the tipis, the graveyards: sap in the trees heats and rises and boils and explodes: a snowstorm of splinters blinds the tribes.

Astride him, whipping, whipping him endlessly, bone arms howling like flutes, the dead man, the furious dead man, and he's laughing as he rides, laughing, cursing, shattering as he rides, he rides dressed in smoke, and he rides.

VIII.

"I wish to repeat this: *Tom Horn was seldom profane.*"

—John C. Coble

I should damn well think not.
John, among
my limited list of friends,
would know:

there was no need
for unpleasant
vocalizations: I had
a cordial relationship

with the earth, and cared
not to sully it
with bloody-minded talk:
those who rode

the plains, the desert and the
lonely range
were serious thinking
men: every one of us

maintained the comfort
of philosophical miles
between us,
and death ain't

changed it.
My mind was too full
of the hard details
that consumed me:

in the touchable world
was what you might
call poetry. God
certainly

was a hands-on
type like myself or
perhaps the Apache Geronimo,
who could be called my friend

and who never cussed
in my hearing, thoughtful

and full of respect
even when he killed:

and if he didn't
always respect the poor
son of a bitch he was
drilling, well

he respected
the larger thing
that was his death.
Our old friend.

I am the Stallion King
I can do anything

Well, what did I expect?
My day was done, as
was the day of
Geronimo

and I myself had took him in:
Nana the Apache captured,
and yours truly
did the deed:

the buffalo dead
and gone.
And men across the many miles
keeled over with a shot in the head.

That's a difficult feat, and to prove
who'd done it, I lay a rock 'neath
each head—a little reminder
of eternal sleep. Lest

you forget.
No room left for the likes
of myself, and I knew
the thing before anyone spoke it.

There were men still needed killing
to trim up
their attitudes,
but not by me.

The Christian state of Wyoming
figured to improve
my comportment
by taking this six feet

and five inches of me
and stretching it
till I was drawn
out thin and quiet

as a late afternoon
shadow.

IX.

They dammed the gorge.
Creeks ran confused: suddenly
fat beyond their shores, nowhere
to flow: no downhill
course: no
voice: no
bed. No
snow
melt
: no
fish
: no
bird
: no
call
: no
rock
: no
gold
: no
milt
: no
frog
: no
eggs
: no
nest
: no
worm
: no
pool
: no
fall
: no
song
: no
more
run.

X.

and Linwood, stripped
of shadows, waited: shutters
clacked in hungry windows,
newspapers bore unheeded news
flew against locked doors—locked
for what? To keep
the turtles out, the
water somehow
waiting?

Dead gunfighters buried
and forgotten
thirteen paces behind
the Square awoke;
two prospectors laid
in a grave by the stream
awoke: dead travelers
from the mountains
poured into the valley
on bony horses.

Soon, slick as paper, the flow wrapped the town.
Mud rose like smoke
from the chimneys.

Robinson Jeffers wrote
not much has yet
died in the West.

Sherman Alexie said:
Yeah? Just ask
Gary Gilmore.

XI.

The News came today.   On tattered pages
they called for a Celebration
of the Stallion King.
It's the third of July: all over town
firecrackers
go off
like skirmishes
bushwhackers
shooting .44's.
And the paper said:

> *Cheyenne, Wyoming hosts the annual Tom Horn Kick & Growl*
> *September 18–20.   Events commemorate the life of notorious assas-*
> *sin Tom Horn, accused of murdering young Willie Nickell in 1901*
> *and hanged for the crime in 1903.*

Tom Horn Kick & Growl.
Tom Horn
        Kick
& Growl.
I'd like to see
one of them say it
to his face.
Those folks think the dead
are so safe.

Tom
     Horn
             Kick

& Growl.

XII.

Years later, I lay in my small tent,
the wildest storm of the year just in from Wyoming
dropping bombs on far piñon, blew
up trees and boulders on the shore.
I shook inside, tent breathing
in panicked gasps, waiting for that
ever-coming rip
that would peel me away
from my small connection
to the dirt.

But the execution was stayed
once more before dawn,
and the judge
black robes across the moon
rode on to Colorado
and beat himself to death
against the Stony Mtns.,
his blood
falling silent
into the gorge.

And here's another one you've probably heard:
Unexpectedly, beneath the last silent skirt
of rain,
came horses.

All around
        they ran
hooves
drumming soil
till it sang.

Their insane screaming
aimed at the lightning
        scrambling
its burning centipede legs
over the hills, cloud-voices
drunk as sailors and cursing
all below.

Dark horses, so dark
I climbed out of my bag to try to see them,
        they tornadoed around me

as I crawled from the tent,
straining now to see: their noise
swooped and whinnied. I felt
their pounding
in the mud:
their feet
running up
against the bottoms
of my feet.

And
I saw there was nothing.

XIII.

The dark itself was galloping.
It ran a circuit north, east, south,
West.   Began
again.
Dogs sounded the alarm: invisible
horses.
Invisible
horses.

I knew
the shadows of the lake
had come for me,
like they have often
chased after you.
I spoke their names
and waited.

They were riding horses
long black horses
quicksilver horses
Oglala horses
burning blue horses
Calvary's horses
skeletal horses
Mexican horses
biblical horses
motorized horses
waterlogged horses
hungry dead horses
screaming dead horses
flying dead horses.
They were riding
invisible horses.

They were riding

invisible horses.

Tell everybody

you know:

the horses

are coming.

V
Final Convocation

And the Wind to Blow Us On

. . . these are the soul cages . . .
                                   —Sting

1.

They put my mother and me both
of us in a cage.   I'd arranged with the zoo
for this one day: a tour, a treat
for her in her loneliness
after my retreat to New
England's tawny Falls, Walden
Pond the size

                    of my rippling dreams.
My mother's solitude hammered her
into shapes I could not fathom—
strange new fears, hair as thin
as late summer's long-grass
in Concord's Great Meadow,
burned by first frost's
slyest licks.   Grayed
and dried and thin
upon the ground
of her head.

Zookeepers led us from cage to cage,
back-door gates swayed wide for us,
and in we strolled, arm-in-
arm, at last, the couple
she always hoped we
could be.   Me
in place of
all those
lost

        men who tore her eyes.
And in each cage, a new
creature, fierce
in its self, there
and not there.   Submitting
to our tentative palms,
full in their feathers and fur, yet
gone—running

77

on landscapes

          that whispered inside
from their blood. My mother's
sad hands hard in mine.

And I too was gone running
inside.

2.

This

a poem she wrote:

          Nearing seventy
          Coming into harbor
          After a stormy crossing
          Blown before the wind
          Hatches battened down
          Fires banked or out
          Now swinging gently
          At anchor
          All fear and sadness
          Washed away
          Pain and sorrow too
          Good memories remain.
          Time now to enjoy
          A book, the colour
          In a glass of wine
          Comfort in a purring cat
          Waiting, serenely and unafraid
          For the tide to turn
          And the wind to
          Blow us on.

3.

The first cage was large, and an emu
strode in, gaunt feathered
dinosaur, eager
to eat my moustache: "She thinks
it's a worm," this from the zookeeper.
My mother scolding: "You bad bird!"

The second cage held a wallaby, small
and hunched, sad

as a fur coat.   "You sweet
thing," my mother said.

The third cage had a violent
small dog, red
from the veldt, afraid
of me.   Afraid
of men.

In the fourth cage, a cheetah, one
long yellow-orange muscle.   His tail
imperious, tufted, bade us enter.
Along his flank, dark mouths gaped, open as if
to eat the wind; shadowy rosettes.
"Give him your hand," the zookeeper said,
"palm flat to his mouth.   Don't
offer him your fingers or
he might eat them."

And my mother, fearless now—after all
this was just a cat—scratched him
like a tabby and like
a tabby he lay over
on one side, licked
her hand and purred

and purred.

This

one of five times
in her last five years
I ever saw her
happy.

4.

My mother's journal.

Sept 29

dont know why, just cant seem to get it together—feel I
wont live much longer—Papers—things—clothes etc all
need working on—House needs a good cleaning + waxing—
yard horrible—I cant do it!   Cough very bad—heart very irregular—
wake up with head + face aching every day—
my life is hell—surely there wont be another one in the
next world—I am ready to leave this one—NOW!

5.

By now, most of those animals
are probably dead.

6.

Alone in her bed for quiet days.
The pale box of the house pulled tight.
Sunlight swept the room.   One
soft clear window-shaft perfect, still,
searched out her dreamy frown
against the feather pillow.   Beside her,
a cookbook, and a Bible.

Each night pulled close around her
a blanket of stars, cooling her skin.
No sound in the house but the panicked cat
at the end of her bed, calling,
calling, stupidly calling
her to awake.

They broke in.
Caught her in the earliest drift
of her terminal dream.
Right hand curled
around her last breath.

And now we feed her
to the flames.

7.

Caged
by everything
she hated

35
years
exiled

to California's
dread sun,
she

escaped, got
away at last—
Cape May,

New Jersey
in a box eight
inches high by

eight inches
wide by eight
inches long.

My mother
just five pounds
of seashells.

8.

Mother, please forgive
the days alone, the
empty rooms
where you
waited.

The harbor calm, silent,
journey over.
And do not be afraid.

Tomorrow on the stormy coast
the Atlantic waves that called
from girlhood's beach
will take you
out, the charging

cheetahs in the waves
will run you
through the gates,
past the shoreline's rocks
to Africa, beyond
the Cape of
Good Hope.

You must go alone
among that restless surf
but soon enough
my wind comes too
and turns
and blows me on.

for Phyllis
1916–1990

Here's the Dream

Here's the dream: Steve McQueen isn't dead, and he holds
my arms as I straddle the splintered rail of a rodeo chute.
The Brahma bull's name is Whirlwind: he's moon-eyed, mammoth,
hump-backed, wild. I am afraid. Shag on his neckline stinks
of sage, salt. His tail jitters on the wood: I spin rope
around my fist, nod once, terse as a movie cowpoke.

William Holden isn't dead. He creaks the chute-gate wide:
Whirlwind corkscrews out, but before he bucks, he stops dead-
still. He stares at the bruised sides of the mountains.
He looks back at me. Eye to eye we decide. He blows steam.
We stampede 2000 tourists out of the stands: we take the
stairs in a sea-swell rhythm: we fly over fences, stomp
up the interstate, leap the river, run the highlands, cruise
the coast, hard hooves rattatat and sparking, lighting fire
in flowers left to dry in desert boneyards.

Here's the dream: I ride this killer bull full-bore
through a land where no one dies.